5/97

Our Oceans

Our Oceans

Experiments and Activities in Marine Science

BY PAUL FLEISHER
Illustrated by Patricia Keeler

The Millbrook Press
Brookfield, Connecticut

To Joseph H. Fleisher,
my first science teacher

Photographs courtesy of Peter Arnold, Inc.: cover (© Brian
Yarvin); NASA: p. 6; E. R. Degginger, Earth Scenes/Animals
Animals: p. 10; Photo Researchers: pp. 18 (Franz Lazi), 48
(Douglas Faulkner), 64 (Frances Gohier); Woods Hole Ocean-
ographic Institution: pp. 32, 40.
Photographs of experiments by Francis McCall

Library of Congress Cataloging-in-Publication Data
Fleisher, Paul.
Our oceans : experiments and activities in marine science / by
Paul Fleisher ; illustrated by Patricia Keeler.
p.   cm.
Includes bibliographical references and index.
Summary: An introduction to marine science that
includes activities and experiments to explore the ocean.
ISBN 1-56294-575-0
1. Oceanography—Experiments—Juvenile literature.
[1. Oceanography—Experiments.   2. Experiments.]   I. Keeler,
Patricia A., ill.   II. Title.
GC21.5.F57   1995
551.46′0078—dc20   95-1962   CIP   AC

Contents

Introduction

Seen from space, our world is a blue ball covered with water. The oceans are our planet's largest feature by far. Less than a third of our planet's surface is dry land. The rest—about 70 percent—is covered with water.

The science that studies the ocean environment is called marine science or oceanography. Marine science is a combination of many traditional sciences, including chemistry, physics, geology, biology, meteorology, and ecology.

In 1872 the first voyage planned especially for ocean study began. The British research ship *Challenger* traveled almost 70,000 miles (112,650 kilometers), measuring currents, temperatures, ocean depth, and the chemistry of seawater along the way. Among their many findings, *Challenger* scientists discovered that seawater contains the same chemicals worldwide. The expedition also found almost 5,000 previously unknown species of undersea animals!

In the twentieth century, interest in marine science grew tremendously. Thousands of expeditions gathered information about the oceans. World-famous research labs such as the Woods Hole Oceanographic Institute in Massachusetts and the Scripps Institute in California specialize in the study of the oceans. Many universities now offer degrees in marine science. Modern technology, including SONAR, SCUBA, submersible water craft, and satellite photography, helped expand our knowledge of the oceans.

But marine scientists have much more to learn. There are still new and unexpected discoveries every year. For example, undersea biologists recently discovered an entirely new group of animals living in the deepest parts of the sea. These creatures use the heat and chemicals from volcanic vents as their only energy source. Until a few years ago, no one even imagined that such creatures existed.

The oceans are huge. Even at the end of the twentieth century they are largely unexplored. But learning more about them is an important goal. Governments need to know more about the oceans for economic and military purposes. Oceanography is important to businesses that must transport products across the seas. Fisheries need to understand the life cycles of the species they catch. Some ocean creatures may provide solutions to human medical problems. The oceans surely contain other resources that we don't even know about yet.

Most important, life on earth could not exist without a healthy ocean environment. In order to protect and preserve the world's oceans, we must first understand them more completely.

Marine science will be an exciting and important field of study for years to come.

In the pages that follow, you'll read about the science of the ocean environment. You'll find out how seawater behaves and what chemicals are included in this salty solution. You'll learn about the motion of waves and currents and how the oceans affect the world's weather. You'll read about the ocean floor and the valuable resources that the sea holds for human life. And as you read on, you'll find lots of experiments and activities to help you understand the science of the sea.

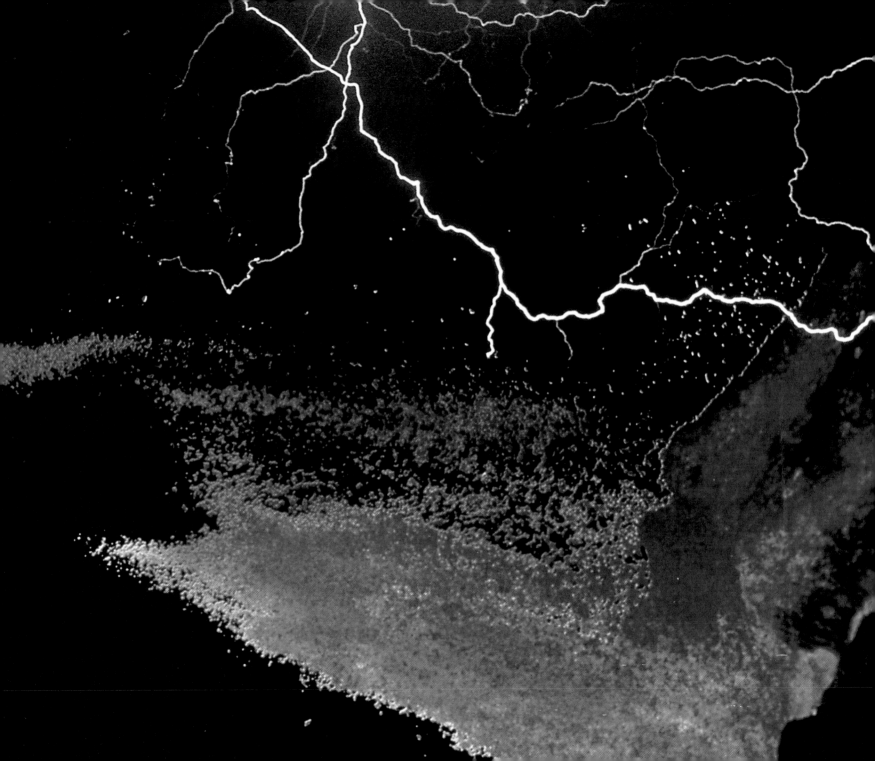

Chapter One

Seawater Chemistry

If you've ever been to the ocean, you know that seawater is *very* salty. Where does this salt come from?

Scientists believe that our planet cooled enough for water to condense and form the oceans about four billion years ago. Since then, rain has dissolved minerals from the land and carried them to the sea. Chemicals from volcanic eruptions have also added to the ocean's salinity (saltiness). When seawater evaporates, the chemicals in it are left behind. Gradually, over millions of years, the salt in the ocean has become more and more concentrated.

SALINITY

The main chemical in seawater is sodium chloride—ordinary table salt. But water can dissolve many different substances. So, seawater contains smaller amounts of many other chemicals, too.

Element	Grams/ Kiloliter	Percentage of dissolved material by weight
Chlorine	19,350	55.1
Sodium	10,760	30.6
Magnesium	1,290	3.7
Sulfur	860	2.4
Calcium	410	1.2
Potassium	390	1.1
Bromine	67	0.2
Carbon	27	0.07
Strontium	8	0.02
Boron	4	0.01
Silicon	3	0.008
Fluorine	1	0.003

Oceanographers always use the metric system for scientific measurements. A gram is about the weight of a paper clip; a liter is a little more than a quart; a kiloliter is 1,000 liters.

Here are the most common chemical elements found in seawater. Notice that chlorine and sodium—the two elements that make up table salt—are at the very top of the list.

In addition to the elements on this list, most of the other chemical elements are also found in seawater—in even smaller amounts. If we had instruments sensitive enough, we could probably find traces of even the rarest chemical elements in seawater.

Make Your Own Seawater

If you live hundreds of miles from the ocean, how do you find seawater to fill a saltwater aquarium or to use in an experiment? Fortunately, you can buy sea salt at almost any pet store.

To create a solution with about the same salinity as seawater, dissolve 35 grams of sea salt in 1 liter of fresh water. This is equivalent to about two level tablespoons of salt dissolved in one quart of water.

Oceanographers often measure salinity in parts per thousand (PPT). The salinity of seawater is about 35 PPT. In other words, a liter of seawater contains about 35 grams of dissolved salts. Remember, this is an average. In coastal areas, where the ocean mixes with fresh water from rivers and streams, the salinity is lower. In hot, dry regions, the ocean loses a lot of water to evaporation. So regions like the Red Sea and the Mediterranean have slightly higher salinities.

DISSOLVED GASES

Both plants and animals need oxygen for respiration (breathing). Ocean water has small amounts of oxygen, nitrogen, and other gases from the air dissolved in it. Gases dissolve into the water at the ocean's surface, where winds and waves mix the air into the water.

See the Air in Water

You can see air dissolved in tap water!

Let water run from a faucet until it's cold. Then fill a clear glass with the water. Set the glass aside for 15 to 30 minutes, until it reaches room temperature. Bubbles of air form on the inner surface of the glass because the warmer water can no longer hold as much dissolved gas.

Gases dissolve best in cold water (just as cold soda holds its fizz better than warm soda). So cold Arctic and Antarctic waters are rich in dissolved oxygen. That helps explain why these frigid regions are surprisingly full of life.

NUTRIENTS

The upper layer of the ocean is populated with uncounted trillions of tiny single-celled algae. Like land plants, algae use sunlight to produce food and oxygen through photosynthesis. And like land plants, they need certain chemical nutrients to grow—the most important being nitrogen, phosphorus, and potassium.

Animals also need these nutrients. Tiny animals eat the algae and use the nutrients for their own growth. Later, these small animals may become food for larger animals. In this way nutrients pass through the food chain from one living thing to another in the ocean environment.

The food chain is essential to the balance of nature.

The chemical cycles that provide nutrients for marine plants and animals are very important to all life on Earth. Let's look at the nitrogen cycle as an example.

Most plants can't use nitrogen directly. They absorb it in the form of chemicals that contain nitrogen, especially nitrates and ammonia. These chemicals enter the oceans in several ways. Some wash into the ocean from the land. Nitrates also form in the atmosphere during lightning strikes and enter the ocean dissolved in rainwater. Some algae also have the special ability to absorb dissolved nitrogen gas from the water and use it directly.

Plants use the nitrogen to make proteins and other compounds that become part of their cells. When animals eat the plants, they use the same nitrogen to build their own bodies. As one animal eats another, the nitrogen and other nutrients are passed along the food chain.

15

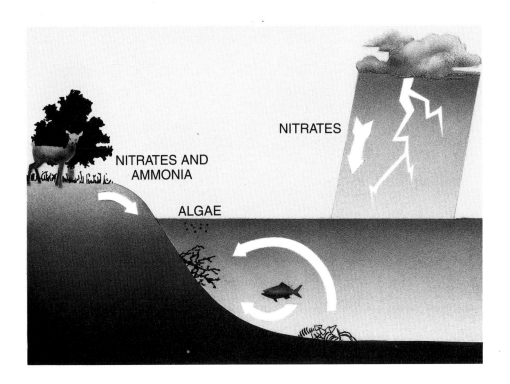

NITRATES

NITRATES AND
AMMONIA

ALGAE

The nitrogen cycle is one of many chemical cycles that are needed to maintain life on Earth.

Not all the nitrogen compounds are digested and used. Urine and digestive waste from animals are rich in nitrates and ammonia. Plants absorb the animal wastes from the water and recycle the nutrients in them. When an animal dies and decays, the nitrogen compounds in its body are released back into the water, where plants can reuse them. This whole process is known as the nitrogen cycle.

Potassium and phosphorus, two other nutrients that are essential for life, have similar cycles in the ocean environment.

The amount of nutrients in seawater is usually quite low. These chemicals are so important to living things that they don't stay in the water for long. Plants quickly absorb them and use them to grow.

In fact, the amount of available nitrogen, potassium, and phosphorus limits how much life a region of the ocean can support. Coastal waters like the Chesapeake Bay are greenish in color because the rich supply of nutrients helps algae grow. On the other hand, the beautiful blue waters around many tropical islands are clear because there are so few nutrients to support the growth of algae.

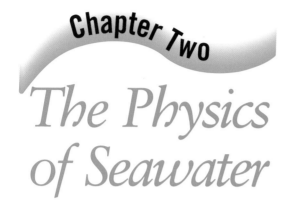

Chapter Two

The Physics of Seawater

Physics is the study of how matter and energy behave. Like any other material, seawater acts in certain ways. It absorbs and releases heat, changes from solid to liquid to gas, exerts pressure, and allows light and sound to pass through it—all in ways that are specific to seawater and different from other materials. These physical properties affect what happens in the oceans.

HEAT AND TEMPERATURE IN OCEAN WATER

Like other materials, water can take three different forms, called "states of matter." These three states are solid, liquid, and gas.

Most materials need extreme temperatures to change states. Consider iron, for example. It must be heated to 2,795 degrees F (1,535 degrees C) before it becomes liquid, and to 5,432 degrees

19

F (3,000 degrees C) before it evaporates into a gas. At the other extreme, nitrogen gas must be cooled to −320 degrees F (−160 degrees C) before it condenses into a liquid and to −210 degrees F (−99 degrees C) before it solidifies.

Water is special. It exists in all three states at normal Earth temperatures. Solid water (ice) forms on the surface of the ocean every winter in Arctic and Antarctic regions. Water in gaseous form is called water vapor. Huge amounts of water evaporate from the surface of the ocean and become part of the air.

It takes heat energy to raise the temperature of any substance. And water can absorb and hold unusually large amounts of heat. Scientists say water has a high "specific heat capacity," which means that it takes a lot of heat to increase the temperature of water just a little bit.

Heat energy is measured in calories. One calorie of heat raises the temperature of a gram of water by one degree C. Compare that with copper, for example. Copper has a much lower heat capacity than water. One calorie will raise the temperature of a gram of copper by 11 degrees!

Because water has such a high specific heat capacity, the ocean is very good at absorbing and holding energy from the sun. As you'll see in Chapter Four, this property rules the world's weather. The ocean is a giant storehouse of solar energy.

It takes even more energy to make a substance change state— from solid to liquid or from liquid to gas. The heat that a substance absorbs as it changes state is called "latent heat." Water absorbs even more energy when it changes state—from solid to liquid or from liquid to gas. It takes 80 calories to melt a gram of ice at 0 degrees into liquid water at the same temperature. That heat doesn't raise the temperature of the water at all—it simply changes its form.

It takes 540 calories to turn a gram of water into water vapor. When water vapor condenses back to liquid form, this latent heat is released back into the atmosphere.

HOW DOES SALT AFFECT THE FREEZING POINT OF SEAWATER?

Materials:

Water, 2 glass jars, salt, ice cubes, thermometer, spoon.

Procedure:

Fill each of the jars with ice cubes. Then add just enough water to cover the cubes. The water level should be about 1 inch (2.5 centimeters) from the top.

Allow the jars of ice water to stand undisturbed for 3 to 5 minutes, until the temperatures of the jars have stabilized. Use the thermometer to measure the temperature of the water in each jar. The water should get no colder than 32 degrees F (0 degrees C).

Now add a teaspoon of salt to one of the jars. Stir thoroughly, dissolving the salt if possible. Then measure the temperature of each jar again. You should notice a change in the one you added salt to. (The other jar is your "control." Continue measuring its temperature, without adding any salt. You can then compare it with the first jar.) *(continued over)*

Repeat this process several more times—adding salt to the experimental jar, stirring, and then measuring the temperature of both jars. Record your results on a chart.

Why does the water temperature drop as you add salt? Think of the liquid water as a reservoir of heat energy that can be used to melt ice. When you add salt, you lower the freezing/melting point of the water. So it takes more heat (drawn from the water) to melt the ice. As the melting ice removes that heat, the temperature of the water goes down.

The more salt that water contains, the lower its temperature.

22

DENSITY

Temperature and salinity both affect the density of seawater. Density is the measure of how much mass a certain volume of matter contains. Iron, for example, is very dense. A cubic centimeter of iron weighs almost 8 grams. Wood, on the other hand, is much less dense. A cubic centimeter of pine wood weighs less than 0.5 gram. Of course, the denser something is, the heavier it feels. (1 cubic centimeter = 0.06 cubic inch; 1 gram = 0.09 ounce)

Because water is such a common and important substance, it is used as the standard for measuring density. A cubic centimeter of water at 4 degrees C (39.2 degrees F) is considered to have a density of exactly 1. An object with a density of less than 1 will float on water. Something with a density higher than 1 will sink.

Water has very unusual density properties. Most substances contract (shrink) and become denser as they cool. As water cools, it also becomes more dense, until it reaches 4 degrees C. But then something unusual happens. When water cools below 4 degrees C, it starts to expand and becomes less dense!

Most substances are also denser in solid form than in liquid form. But solid water—ice—is less dense than liquid water. This is extremely unusual. Because ice is less dense than liquid water, it floats. Thus, sea ice forms on the surface of the water and stays there instead of sinking to the bottom of the ocean.

As ocean water freezes, much of the salt is excluded from (left out of) the ice that forms. The water just below the ice becomes even saltier. This cold, saltier water is denser, so it sinks to the bottom of the ocean. This motion is an important part of the worldwide circulation of deep ocean currents. The water in the deepest parts of the ocean is very cold—just one or two degrees above 32 degrees F (0 degrees C).

WHAT HAPPENS TO THE SALT WHEN SEAWATER FREEZES?

Materials:

Water, salt, 2 clean plastic containers, measuring cup, 2 small glass dishes, a freezer

Procedure:

Dissolve a tablespoon of salt in 2 cups (474 milliliters) of water.

Pour half of the salty water into a second container and place it in the freezer. Wait until a layer of ice forms on the surface of the salt water. Don't let the water freeze entirely.

Remove the ice from the container and rinse it *quickly* under cold tap water. Then put it in the second container and allow it to melt.

Now, compare the taste of the melted "sea ice" with the original salty water you made. You should notice a big difference. Much of the salt will have been excluded from the icy layer. The melted ice should taste much less salty than the original solution.

To complete the experiment, measure equal amounts of the salty water and the melted "sea ice." Pour the samples into the 2 dishes. Set the dishes aside and allow the water to evaporate. Compare the amount of salt that is left behind in each dish.

When frozen seawater is melted, the result is a less salty taste.

Because of differences in density, ocean water forms layers. This process is called "stratification." (Strata are layers.) Just as oil floats on water because it is less dense, warm water will float in a layer above denser cold water. If you've gone swimming in a lake in summer you have felt this stratification. The surface of the water may feel warm, but your legs and feet find colder areas as you wade into deeper water.

This layering is surprisingly stable. Once layers form, they can last for thousands of years! By testing temperatures and chemical composition, marine scientists can identify many different layers of water when they survey the ocean at any single location.

A DEMONSTRATION OF STRATIFICATION

Materials:

A large widemouthed jar with lid, large measuring cup, a fresh hard-cooked egg, water, salt, ladle

Procedure:

Dissolve 1 cup (237 milliliters) of salt in a quart of warm water. Allow the water to cool to room temperature.

Fill the widemouthed jar about two-thirds full of the salt solution. Then float the hard-cooked egg in the jar.

Move the jar very gently, so the water in it stays still.

Carefully float a layer of fresh water on top of the salt water: Hold the ladle at the surface of the water. Slowly pour a gentle

25

Stratification will cause the egg to remain suspended in the jar.

stream of fresh water into it, so it flows out over the surface of the salt water. When the jar is filled, screw on the lid. Gently move the jar to a location where it won't be disturbed.

If you follow these steps carefully, your egg will end up floating in the middle of the jar. The egg is denser than fresh water, so it sinks below that layer. But it is less dense than salt water, so it floats on the salty layer. If you leave the jar undisturbed so that the water isn't stirred, you'll be amazed at how stable it is. The egg will stay suspended in the middle of the jar for a *long* time.

PRESSURE AND DEPTH

We land dwellers live under a pressure of about 1 atmosphere (atm). That's the weight of Earth's atmosphere that presses down on us at sea level. Earth's atmosphere has a pressure of about 14.7 pounds per square inch (a little more than 1 kilogram per square centimeter). That may seem like a lot of pressure. But our bodies are adapted (adjusted) to it, and the pressure pushes in all directions at the same time, so we don't even feel it.

Water is, of course, much heavier than air. The deeper you go in the ocean the more water presses down from above. Pressure in seawater depends only on the depth. It doesn't depend on the size or shape of a submerged object or the shape of the container it is in. At any given depth, anywhere in the ocean, water pressure is the same. Like air pressure, water pressure at any depth pushes equally in all directions—it doesn't just push downward.

SEEING WATER PRESSURE IN ACTION

Materials:

2 empty clear plastic containers (soda bottles, for example), hammer and nail, a basin or sink full of water

Procedure:

Clean each container thoroughly.

Using the hammer and nail, punch a hole in the side of one container, about a quarter of the way up from the bottom. In the second container, punch a hole in the center of the bottom.

Push the first container down into the basin of water, so that it is about three-fourths submerged. Don't let water slosh over the top rim. Watch what happens as the pressure forces water in through the hole. You'll see water being pushed *sideways*.

Repeat the experiment with the second container. This time the pressure pushes the water *up*.

At any depth, water pressure pushes in *all* directions. And it always pushes at right angles to the object it is pushing against.

Pressure can cause water to be pushed in many different directions.

For every 33 feet (10 meters) of depth, water pressure increases by about 1 atmosphere. At 10 meters, the pressure is 2 atmospheres (atm); at 20 meters it is 3 atm; at 30 meters it is 4 atm; and so on. The deepest parts of the ocean are more than 36,000 feet (11,000 meters) below the surface. The pressure at those depths is enormous!

27

Pressure makes it difficult to study the deep ocean environment. Only special scientific instruments can withstand such pressures. Creatures from the ocean depths can't survive if brought to the surface, so learning about their life cycles is also difficult.

SUNLIGHT IN THE OCEAN

Huge amounts of solar energy reach the ocean daily. As sunlight hits the surface, some of it is reflected back. The rest travels through the water until its energy is absorbed as heat.

About 60 percent of all solar energy is absorbed in the top 3 feet (1 meter) of ocean water. In coastal waters cloudy with sediment and microscopic creatures, very little light reaches below a few meters. Even in the clearest ocean water, only about 1 percent of the light goes as deep as about 500 feet (150 meters).

Life in the ocean depends on sunlight. Trillions of single-celled algae form the base of the oceanic food chain. Because they need light for photosynthesis, these algae grow only in the upper layer of the ocean—the top 300 feet (100 meters) or so.

Of all the colors of the rainbow, red light has the least energy. Red light is absorbed in just the first few meters. Other colors of the spectrum travel farther. Blue light has the most energy of visible light. In clear ocean water, blue light may reach more than 3,000 feet (1,000 meters). Beyond that, no sunlight penetrates at all. The ocean depths are forever darker than the darkest night.

Sometimes the ocean looks blue; at other times it appears green. Why is that? The color we see in ocean water comes from light reflected from the surface and from below (called backscattering). High-energy blue light can travel much farther through the water than other colors. Since it travels farther, the blue light is more likely to be reflected back to our eyes before it is absorbed. That reflected light gives clear water its blue color.

Microscopic algae growing in the ocean contain the green pigment chlorophyll, just as plants on land do. Chlorophyll reflects green light but absorbs other colors. So waters rich in floating plant life appear greenish in color instead of blue.

MEASURE WATER CLARITY WITH A SECCHI DISK

Before the invention of electronic light meters, marine scientists used a simple device called a Secchi disk to measure the transparency (clarity) of seawater. Here's how to make and use one:

Materials:

White lid from a 5-gallon plastic bucket, about 12 inches (30 centimeters) in diameter; about 60 feet (20 meters) of ⅛-inch-diameter nylon cord; drill and ¼-inch bit; 2 large steel washers; fishing or other heavy weights; black enamel paint; paint brush

Procedure:

Divide the plastic lid into quarters. Paint two of the quarters black, and leave the other two white, so the black and white quarters alternate. Wait for the paint to dry. *(continued over)*

A Secchi disk is an important marine science instrument, but you can make your own with everyday materials.

29

Drill a hole through the center of the plastic lid. (Ask an adult to help you if you've never used a drill before.) Pass the cord through the hole, and pull about 20 inches (50 centimeters) of it through to the underside. Tie a washer above and below the lid, to hold it tightly in place. On the underside of the lid, tie on enough weights to make the lid sink into the water. Drill a few other holes in the lid to allow water to pass through as it sinks.

Tie a series of knots in the cord at 3-foot (0.9-meter) intervals. The knots will let you measure the depth of the disk.

To measure the transparency of water, slowly lower the disk into the water. Stop as soon as you can no longer see the disk. Then use the knots in the cord to measure how deep the disk is at that point. You can use your Secchi disk readings to compare the transparency of water at different locations in your area.

SOUND IN THE OCEAN

Sound travels about 5 times faster in water than in air. Sound waves travel through air at about 1,115 feet (340 meters) per second; in seawater they travel at about 5,000 feet (1,530 meters) per second. The exact speed of sound in seawater depends on temperature, salinity, and pressure.

Ships and submarines use SONAR (*so*und *na*vigation and *r*anging) to locate submerged objects. SONAR detectors produce sharp pings that travel through the water. The sound bounces off objects and reflects back to a listening device. This SONAR detector calculates the direction and distance of the reflecting objects.

The information is then plotted on a chart or video screen. Much of what we know about the shape of the ocean bottom has been learned using SONAR.

Many ocean creatures use sound to communicate. Whales and dolphins communicate with squeaks, clicks, grunts, whistles, and even tones, or songs. Sound travels so well through the water that some whale songs can be heard for thousands of miles. Dolphins also use sound to locate prey by listening for echoes of the noises they make—much like a SONAR detector.

Fish have a highly developed sense organ called the lateral line that picks up vibrations in the water. This helps them locate prey and avoid predators. Fish and shrimp also make a variety of clicks and grunts—perhaps to locate one another or find prey. The underwater world can be quite a noisy place!

HEAR SOUND THROUGH WATER WITHOUT GETTING WET

Materials:

Water, freezer-weight zipper-style plastic bag, tuning fork

Procedure:

Fill the plastic bag with water. Zip it closed, eliminating as much air as possible.

Hold the bag to your ear. Have someone tap the tuning fork and then hold the end of it to the bag. You should hear the tone quite clearly—much more clearly than through the air. Try listening to other sounds through the water-filled bag as well.

Chapter Three

The Ocean Floor

Is the bottom of the ocean flat and featureless or are there mountains and valleys similar to those on land?

Scientists who study Earth's structure are called geologists. Marine geologists have taken depth measurements, collected samples from the ocean floor, and even visited the deep ocean bottom with submersible craft. They now have a good idea of what Earth's crust is like under the oceans.

Near the edges of the continents the oceans are shallow and the bottom is fairly flat. This region—from 0 to about 450 feet (130 meters) deep—is called the continental shelf. In some places the continental shelf is more than 1,000 miles (1,700 kilometers) wide, in others it is only about half a mile (about 1 kilometer) wide. The average width of the continental shelf is about 50 miles (75 kilometers).

At the edges of the continental shelf the ocean bottom drops off more steeply. Geologists call this area the continental slope. It

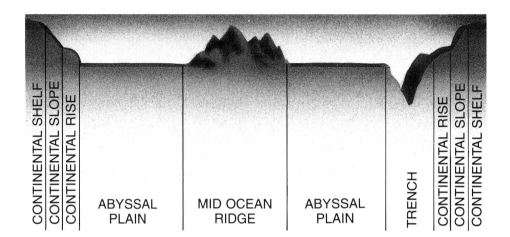

CONTINENTAL SHELF
CONTINENTAL SLOPE
CONTINENTAL RISE

ABYSSAL PLAIN

MID OCEAN RIDGE

ABYSSAL PLAIN

TRENCH

CONTINENTAL RISE
CONTINENTAL SLOPE
CONTINENTAL SHELF

Just like Earth's surface, the ocean floor contains geologic regions as well.

descends to a depth of about 2 miles (3.5 kilometers). At the base of the continental slope is the continental rise. This is the region where Earth's crust begins to rise up from the ocean depths toward the land far above. At the continental rise, sediment from the continents and the waters around them is especially deep.

Much of the ocean bottom is relatively flat and very deep—about 2.5 miles (4 kilometers) or deeper. This is known as the abyssal plain. In various places on the abyssal plain, underwater mountains called seamounts rise toward the surface. Some of these mountains are tall enough to rise above the surface to form islands.

Near the center of the Atlantic, Pacific, and Indian oceans is a long chain of undersea mountains called the mid-ocean ridge. These mountains cover about one third of the entire ocean floor. They rise as much as 1¼ miles (2 kilometers) or more above the abyssal plain.

In many places the mid-ocean ridge is active with volcanoes and earthquakes. Scientists now believe the seafloor is slowly expanding in both directions from these mid-ocean ridges. The sea floor enlarges as volcanic action creates new rock along the ridge. The seafloor is spreading at a rate of ½ to 4 inches (1 to 10 centimeters) per year.

Geologists now believe that Earth's crust is divided into about 30 large plates. These plates float on a layer of denser rock deep below Earth's surface. Because of the great pressure of the plates above, this hot, dense rock can flow very slowly, like road tar on a hot day. The continents float along with the plates. Over millions of years, as the seafloor spreads, their positions on the globe have gradually changed.

Look at a world map. You'll see that the east coast of South America looks as though it would fit neatly with the west coast of Africa. Geologists believe that about 200 million years ago all the continents were connected. But spreading of the sea floor slowly pushed them apart. This process is still continuing today.

In some places where the seafloor meets the edge of the continents, this slow spreading pushes one plate down under the edge of another. These areas are called subduction zones. These zones create the deepest parts of the ocean, called trenches. The Mariannas Trench in the western Pacific is the ocean's deepest point. It is almost 7 miles (11 kilometers) below the surface.

Volcanoes often erupt near subduction zones, and earthquakes are also common as one plate slides beneath another. The earthquakes and volcanoes of Japan, coastal Alaska, and the west coast of South America are thought to be caused by subduction.

A MODEL CROSS-SECTION OF THE OCEAN FLOOR

Materials:

A piece of blue posterboard, 18 by 24 inches (46 by 61 centimeters); a piece of brown or gray construction paper of the same size; pencil, scissors, glue, marker

Procedure:

On the construction paper, lightly pencil an outline of a typical seafloor profile, like the one in the drawing on page 32. Make sure you include all the following features: continental shelf, continental slope, continental rise, abyssal plain, seamount, mid-ocean ridge, and trench.

Once you're satisfied with the outline you've drawn, carefully cut it out and glue it onto the posterboard. Finally, label all the different features you've included.

For a more ambitious project, make a 3-dimensional model using papier-mâché or modeling clay.

ISLAND FORMATION

Islands form in a number of different ways. Many islands are volcanic in origin. Huge amounts of lava can pour from undersea volcanoes, forming mountains that may eventually rise above the surface of the ocean. The Hawaiian Islands and Iceland are examples of islands that formed in this way.

Other islands are formed by the growth of coral. Corals are small animals related to jellyfish. They have stinging tentacles that they use to capture prey from the waters around them. Unlike jellyfish, corals live in huge colonies attached to a solid surface. They must live in shallow water, because each animal has a special algae—called zooxanthellae—that grow inside the coral. These algae need sunlight to grow. Zooxanthellae produce much of the food that corals need to survive.

Each coral animal builds a small limestone cup in which it lives. When it dies, the limestone is left behind. Other corals grow on top of it.

Over many years, corals build up great reefs. If the sea level drops, these reefs are exposed. They become limestone islands. The Bahamas and the Florida Keys were created in this way. Corals also build atolls, ring-shaped islands around the tops of volcanic seamounts.

Other islands are produced as wind and waves pile up mounds of sand in shallow coastal waters. These barrier islands start as underwater sandbars. But the waves may gradually build the sandbar into a new island. The island gathers more and more sand carried by the wind and waves. Grasses and other plants take root. The plants help hold the sand in place and create windbreaks that capture even more sand. Changes in sea level and great storms can also expose or drown barrier islands. Miami Beach, the Outer Banks in North Carolina, and Atlantic City, New Jersey, are all barrier islands.

SEDIMENTS

The ocean floor is almost entirely covered with thick layers of mudlike sediments. These small particles drift down from the upper layers of the ocean in a fine, steady rain. It can take a long time for sediments to finally reach the ocean floor. A grain of sand takes about two days to fall from the surface to the abyssal plain. Grains of clay are much smaller, so they can take fifty or more years to drift down to the ocean bottom!

Sediment builds up slowly. In most parts of the ocean, sediments deepen at the rate of a few millimeters a year. (1 inch = 25.4 millimeters) But over millions of years, that adds up. In most areas of the deep ocean, the layer of sediment is from 1,500 to more than 3,000 feet (500 to 1,000 meters) thick!

Where does all this sediment come from? Much of it is the result of erosion. Rivers wash about 20 billion tons of sand, silt, and clay into the ocean each year. Winds also carry fine particles of stone and soil into the air; this material later falls into the ocean or is carried down in rainfall. Ash from volcanic eruptions also adds to ocean sediments.

Living creatures are another important source of sediment. Trillions of microscopic creatures—diatoms, radiolarians, and others—live in the ocean's surface waters. As they die, their tiny shells create biological sediments called oozes. The bodies of larger animals such as fish also contribute to these sediments.

Chemical reactions in seawater also produce some sediments. And believe it or not, dust from space—meteorites—adds about 30,000 tons of sediment to the ocean each year.

The weight of the sediment on the ocean floor squeezes the deeper layers together, forming sedimentary rock. As Earth's plates shift, these rocks may lift up to form new land. Some sedimentary rocks can be found in mountains thousands of feet above sea level. They may even contain the fossils of sea creatures that have been extinct for hundreds of millions of years.

SIMULATED SEDIMENTARY ROCK

Here's how to simulate the formation of sedimentary rock:

Materials:

Large plastic bowl, ½ cup (119 milliliters) of sand and mud, handful of small pebbles, ½ cup (119 milliliters) mortar mix (from hardware store), 2 cups (474 milliliters) water

Procedure:

Put the sand, mud, and pebbles into the empty bowl. Add the mortar mix. Then add the water.

Stir the mixture thoroughly. Put the bowl in a sunny location where it won't be disturbed. After a day, the sediments will settle to the bottom. Carefully pour off the clear water. Then put the bowl back in the sun. After a few more days, the water will evaporate completely, leaving a piece of simulated sedimentary rock.

Remember, real sedimentary rock only forms over millions of years, as the weight of more and more sediment squeezes the tiny particles of clay, sand, and biological ooze together.

Your handmade sedimentary rock shows what happens to rock over millions of years.

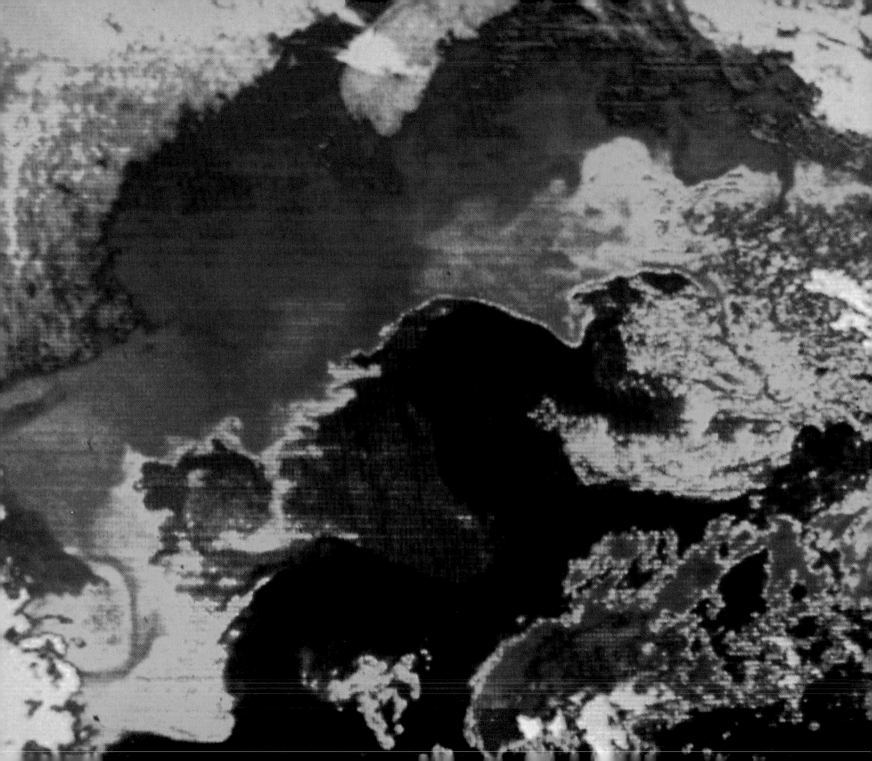

Chapter Four

Ocean Currents and Global Climate

The oceans are the most important influence on the world's weather. This is true for three main reasons.

First, oceans receive most of the solar energy that reaches Earth's surface. Solar energy is the force that powers the world's weather. When sunlight hits Earth, some of it is reflected back out into space. But most of it is absorbed and turned into heat. Since 70 percent of the world is covered by water, most of the solar energy that reaches Earth's surface is absorbed by the oceans.

Second, as we saw in Chapter Two, water can absorb tremendous amounts of heat. So the oceans become a giant storehouse of solar energy. Some of that solar energy raises the temperature of the water. Global wind patterns—also powered by solar energy—create great surface currents like the Gulf Stream. These currents carry solar heat from warmer regions to cooler ones, making the world's climate much more moderate than it would otherwise be.

Coastal New England, for example, has much milder winters than inland areas at the same latitude, because of the warming effects of the Gulf Stream.

The currents also carry colder Arctic waters back toward the tropical regions of the globe where they are warmed once again. This global circulation of currents spreads solar energy more evenly around the world.

Third, solar energy evaporates huge amounts of water from the ocean surface. The ocean loses about 3 feet (1 meter) of water each year to evaporation. That's a lot of water! That water is replaced when the evaporated water condenses and falls back to Earth as rain.

It takes heat energy to evaporate water. The water vapor carries that latent heat with it into the atmosphere. Latent heat is a form of potential energy.

When the water vapor later condenses, it releases the heat into the atmosphere. This provides the energy to power Earth's storm systems.

Winds may carry water vapor thousands of miles before it eventually condenses into clouds and rain. This also distributes solar energy more evenly around the globe.

THE CORIOLIS EFFECT

Earth rotates from west to east on its axis. This movement creates a surprising effect: If you were to look at a globe marked with wind direction and ocean currents, you would see that moving water and air bend to the right in the Northern Hemisphere. This gives ocean currents and winds a clockwise spin. This motion is known as the Coriolis effect. In the Southern Hemisphere, the Coriolis effect turns moving air and water currents to the left. So south of the equator, winds and currents move in a counterclockwise direction.

Here's how it works:

Everything on Earth's surface, including the oceans and the atmosphere, rotates to the east along with Earth itself. Earth's surface moves fastest at the equator, because that's where Earth's diameter is greatest. As you move away from the equator toward the poles, the distance around the globe decreases, so the speed of rotation decreases as well.

Now imagine an object moving northward from the equator. In addition to its northward motion, it is already moving eastward at almost 1,050 miles (1,690 kilometers) per hour, along with everything else at the equator. But as it moves north, the surface it travels across is moving a bit more slowly. So the object's extra eastward speed makes it curve to the right, in a clockwise direction.

The effect also applies to anything moving southward. Imagine standing at the North Pole and firing a rocket directly south. As the rocket travels southward in a straight line, Earth turns eastward beneath it at a faster and faster rate. As a result, to a viewer on Earth's surface the rocket seems to be curving to the right.

South of the equator, Earth's motion has a similar effect. But in the Southern Hemisphere both winds and currents turn in a counterclockwise direction.

Simulating the Coriolis Effect helps demonstrate the effect of Earth's rotation on moving objects.

SIMULATING THE CORIOLIS EFFECT

Materials:

Washable marker, globe of the world

Procedure:

Place the globe on a table. Place your marker at the North Pole. Have a helper turn the globe to the east while you draw a line straight down toward the South Pole. Use the frame that supports the globe to guide your marker in a straight path.

Even though the line you draw is perfectly straight, you'll see that its path will curve in an S shape. The line will turn clockwise in the Northern Hemisphere and counterclockwise in the Southern Hemisphere.

UPWELLING

Along some coastlines, winds push the surface water away from the shore. When this happens, deeper waters rise to replace the water moved by the wind. This process is known as upwelling.

The deeper waters contain more dissolved nutrients. When the nutrients reach the surface, they increase the growth of algae. Animals that depend on algae for food also thrive. So regions of upwelling are rich in sea life. Upwelling is very important for the world's food supply. Although they make up a tiny fraction of the ocean, upwelling regions produce half of the world's fish harvest.

The ocean affects local weather patterns as well as the global climate.

On hot days at the seashore, there is almost always a cooling breeze blowing in from the ocean. Remember, in Chapter Two we saw that water has a much greater heat capacity than most other materials. As a result, sunlight warms the land faster than it warms the water. The air above the land is also warmed, and it rises. As this warm air rises, cooler air from the nearby ocean rushes in to take its place, causing onshore breezes.

At night, the opposite is often true. The land cools more quickly than the water. As the comparatively warmer air above the ocean rises, cooler air from the land moves in, creating off-shore breezes. Many people visit the seashore each summer to take advantage of these cooling ocean breezes.

Water's ability to absorb and hold heat also keeps winter temperatures milder near the shore. Along both the eastern and western seacoasts of the United States, for example, regions near the ocean often get rain at the same time that inland areas are getting sleet and snow.

The humidity from evaporating ocean water can also create local rain showers. Tropical islands and coastal areas often have afternoon showers, for example. Moist air rises up as it is warmed by the land. As it rises into the upper atmosphere, this air becomes cooler again. The water vapor condenses to form clouds and rain. Seafarers know they are approaching a tropical island long before it comes into view, because they can see the clouds rising high above it on an otherwise clear day.

As water temperature rises, the colored water will rise to the surface.

TEMPERATURE-DRIVEN CURRENTS IN YOUR KITCHEN

You can see how differences in temperature create movement in the ocean and the atmosphere—called convection currents—with this simple demonstration.

Materials:

Water, liquid food coloring, ice cube tray or small plastic container, Pyrex measuring cup or beaker, plastic drinking straw, heat source (hot plate or electric stove)

Procedure:

Mix a few drops of food coloring into an ounce of water. Freeze the colored water in your refrigerator's freezer.

Fill the measuring cup with cold water. Allow it to reach room temperature. To keep the water still, don't move the container.

Float the colored ice in the room-temperature water. Watch what happens to the cold colored water as the ice melts.

You should see streamers of dense cold water sink to the bottom through the warmer water. Similar sinking happens in the ocean when surface waters cool during fall and winter.

Follow up:

(Ask an adult for help with this.) Fill the measuring cup or beaker with tap water. Place it on the hot plate or stove. Wait 10 minutes so the water becomes completely still. *(continued over)*

Put the drinking straw into the bottle of food coloring. Then put your finger firmly over the top end of the straw. This will hold some of the dye in the straw when you remove it from the bottle.

Very gently put the straw down into the measuring cup. When the end of the straw is at the bottom of the cup, release your finger. This will allow some of the dye to seep out of the straw and color the water at the bottom of the cup. Put your finger back over the end of the straw and gently remove it from the water.

Now turn the burner to a low temperature and watch what happens to the colored water. As the water warms, it becomes less dense. You will see the colored water rise toward the surface.

RAIN-FORMING IMPORTANCE OF SALT PARTICLES

In order to condense into droplets, water vapor needs a nucleus, or "seed particle," to condense around. This nucleus can be a bit of dust. But it is most often a microscopic bit of sea salt! As ocean waves foam and break, they throw billions of small droplets into the air. These droplets often evaporate completely before they fall back into the ocean. This leaves behind tiny salt particles. The particles are so light they don't fall back into the water. Instead, they are carried into the air by the gentlest of winds. In the upper atmosphere, these particles later form the nuclei that rain droplets form around.

47

Chapter Five

Waves and Tides

The surface of the ocean is in constant motion. Waves of all sizes, from tiny ripples to huge storm-driven monsters that can break a ship in two, are always moving across the waters.

Where do these waves come from, and what scientific rules govern their behavior?

WIND WAVES

With the exception of tsunamis (see page 57) and tidal waves, all ocean waves get their energy from the wind. Wind blowing across the water starts tiny ripples in motion. As the wind continues, the waves grow larger.

The size of waves depends on three things: wind speed; duration—the length of time that the wind continues to blow;

and fetch—the distance over which the wind is blowing. As any one of these increases, the waves get larger.

It's just what you would expect to happen. A 20-mile (32-kilometer)-per-hour wind makes bigger waves than a 10-mile (16-kilometer)-per-hour wind. A wind that blows steadily for 12 hours creates larger waves than one that blows for 6 hours. And a wind that blows across a distance of 100 miles (160 kilometers) causes bigger waves than one that only blows across a 50-mile (80-kilometer) fetch.

How big can wind-driven ocean waves get? Great storms may generate ocean waves 100 feet (30 meters) high—as high as a 10-story building!

Waves in a stormy or windy area can be wild and disorganized. These types of waves are called a sea. As waves travel outward from the storm, they separate into long, smooth waves called swells.

PARTS OF A WAVE

Every wave has a highest and lowest point. The high point of a wave is called the crest. The low point is called the trough. When we think of waves, we usually think of crests. But you can't have a crest without a trough. It takes both to make a complete wave.

The distance between two crests is called the wavelength. The height of a wave, from trough to crest, is called the wave's amplitude. And the time it takes for a complete wave to pass by is called

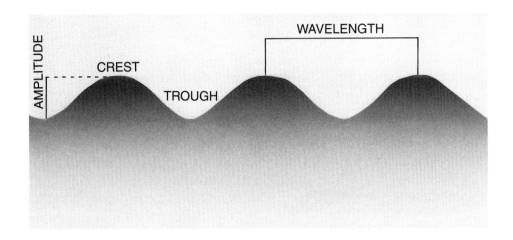

Waves occur continuously in the ocean.

the period. Because waves of all sizes are usually mixed together, it is difficult to make exact measurements of wavelength, amplitude, and period on the open ocean.

WAVE BEHAVIOR

Although waves move through the water, the water itself hardly moves at all! Waves carry the wind's energy through the water. But individual water particles remain pretty much in place; they just bob up and down in small circles as the waves pass by. It's a good thing this is true. Otherwise, large amounts of water would pile up along the shore.

51

A SIMPLE WAVE PROJECTOR

Materials:

A clear glass baking dish, water, an overhead projector and a projection screen (your school will have these), a couple of pencils, a box of paraffin (available at any grocery store)

Procedure:

Place the baking dish on the projector and fill it with an inch or so of water. Set up the projection screen and turn on the projector.

A wave projector can help you observe the properties of waves.

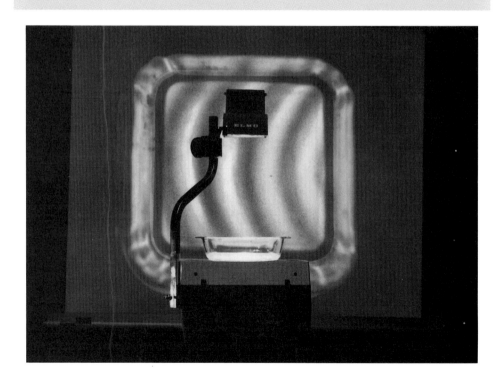

Here is one way to see diffusion. Another way is to toss a pebble into a pond or lake.

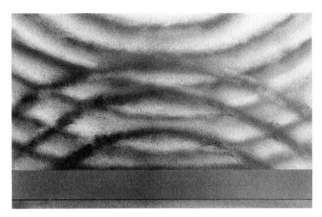

Reflection is easier to observe on sunny days, when the object under the water can absorb the sun's rays.

Now tap the water gently with a pencil. The waves in the water will be projected on the screen as moving bands of light and dark. The crests and troughs of the waves act as lenses. They focus the light to produce this effect.

Use your wave projector to see these properties of waves:

Diffusion: Waves spread out in all directions from a source. Tap the surface of the water with the pencil. You will see the waves traveling outward in ever-widening circles.

Reflection: Waves bounce back from obstacles. When an ocean wave hits a seawall or breaks on a beach, some of the wave's energy is reflected back in the opposite direction. Put a block of paraffin in the water of your wave projector to serve as

53

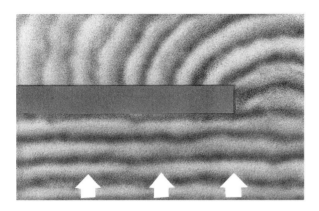

Even obstacles cannot deter waves from their paths.

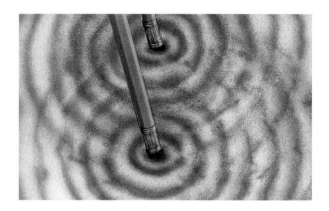

Interference looks harmless here, but when it occurs during ocean storms it can create towering waves.

an obstacle. Tap the water several inches away from the block and watch the waves reflect from it.

Diffraction: Waves bend around obstacles. Ocean waves that meet jetties or other objects in their paths curve around the edges of those objects and continue traveling forward. Watch what happens as the waves pass the ends of the paraffin block. You'll see them curve around the block and continue on the other side.

Interference: Interesting things happen when two waves meet each other. Where a crest meets a crest, an extra-high crest forms. Where trough meets trough, the result is an extra-deep trough. And where trough meets crest, the waves cancel each other out, creating an area of flat water. Tap the water gently in two different spots, using two pencils. You'll see an overlapping series of light and dark regions called an interference pattern. It's interference—when the crests of two large waves meet—that creates monster waves during ocean storms.

Refraction: Water waves refract, or slow down and bend, as they travel through shallower water. Refraction is difficult to see in our simple wave tank, but you can try. Prop up one end of the tank by sliding small books under the corners. Now the water in one end is shallower, while the other is deeper. Generate waves in the deep end of the tank and watch what happens as they approach the shallow end. You may be able to see that the slower-moving waves at the shallow end get closer together.

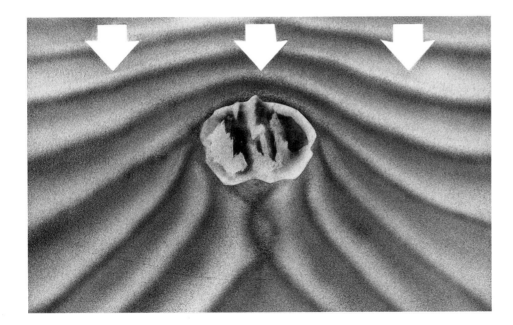

Refraction means that waves will always roll in toward the beach, no matter what direction they are coming from.

Here's one interesting result of refraction: Imagine yourself on a small island. The wind is blowing from the east, so the waves approach the island from that direction. But no matter where you are on the island—east, west, north or south—the waves still roll in toward the beach. Waves always break toward the beach, no matter what direction they approach the island from! But why?

Since waves travel more slowly in shallow water, they curve around as they approach land. The part of the wave nearer shore slows down, allowing the part in deeper water to "catch up" until it is parallel to the shoreline.

On the open ocean, large waves can travel for thousands of miles in long, smooth swells. But as waves approach a shoreline their behavior changes. These waves are called surf, or breakers. At a certain depth—one half of its wavelength—a wave begins to be affected by the bottom. It slows down and begins to pile up into a breaker. As the water gets even shallower, the wave can no longer support itself. Finally it breaks, tumbling over in an avalanche of foam.

When waves break along a shoreline, they can create very localized currents. One of these is called undertow. Undertow is simply the water from a breaking wave flowing back down the beach to the ocean. Bathers caught in an undertow may panic, thinking they are being pulled out to sea. But undertows never travel more than a few feet before they disappear.

Another local current is called a rip current. This is also a pathway for water to return after being brought to shore in breakers. Rip currents travel farther than an undertow. But if a swimmer simply rides with them, he or she will quickly be carried to calmer water and can then swim back to shore.

Sometimes waves break at an angle to the beach. This creates long shore currents, or cross currents. Over time, these currents can carry large amounts of sand from one part of a beach to another.

TSUNAMIS

Tsunamis are huge waves created by undersea earthquakes, volcanic eruptions, or landslides. They are sometimes—incorrectly—called "tidal waves." Earthquakes can cause a sudden shift in Earth's crust beneath the sea. This motion sends out powerful, rapidly moving waves in all directions. Tsunamis have extremely long wavelengths—100 miles (160 kilometers) or more between crests. They can travel through the ocean at speeds of 500 miles (800 kilometers) an hour.

Tsunami means "harbor wave" in Japanese. Tsunamis were given this name because their destructive effects are only seen in shallow waters. On the open ocean, tsunamis are hardly noticeable, because their wavelengths are so long. The water rises only a few feet as a tsunami passes by. But when they approach shore, tsunamis slow down and pile up into monstrous waves that can be 60 feet (18 meters) high or more!

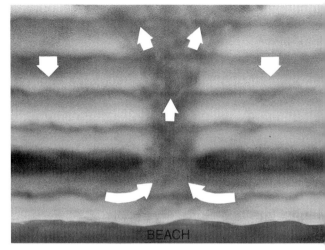

Rip currents are really the pathways water takes back to sea after it has hit the shore.

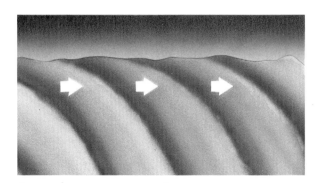

Longshore currents often create erosion—the result of moving and redepositing large amounts of sand.

Tsunamis are most common in the Pacific, because far more earthquakes happen there. They also occur in other parts of the oceans but much more rarely.

Tsunamis can be extremely destructive. Hawaii, Japan, and other places threatened by these waves have tsunami warning systems. Scientists listen for undersea earthquakes with seismographic equipment. If they suspect a tsunami is coming, people are told to leave coastal areas quickly.

TIDES

Earth and the moon attract each other with gravitational force. This force holds the moon in orbit around Earth. The moon and Earth actually swing around each other. As they revolve they pivot around a point about 2,920 miles (4,700 kilometers) from the center of Earth.

The moon's gravitational force pulls on the ocean's water, creating a bulge or wave that we call the tide. At the same time, on the opposite side of Earth another wave forms. This wave is produced by centrifugal force—the force created as the moon and Earth swing around each other.

Earth also rotates, or spins, on its axis at the same time. As it rotates, Earth's crust moves beneath the tidal bulges. So each of the tides travels completely around the globe in about one day.

The sun's gravity also causes tidal motion. But because the sun is much farther away, it affects the tide less strongly than the moon does.

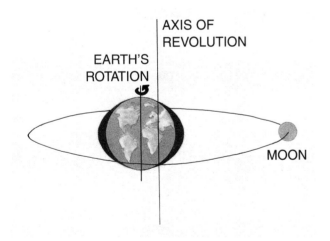

AXIS OF REVOLUTION

EARTH'S ROTATION

MOON

Every tide completes an around-the-world journey in one day.

Ocean in a Bottle

Here's a decorative craft project that will let you enjoy watching the motion of waves whenever you pick it up. You will need a clear glass bottle with a cap that seals tightly (a soda bottle will do), mineral oil (available at any drugstore), water, and blue food coloring.

Clean the bottle thoroughly. Then fill it about half full with fresh water. Add a few drops of the blue food coloring.

Fill the bottle all the way to the top with mineral oil. Screw the cap on tightly. To prevent spills, you can seal the cap with a few turns of clear tape.

The clear oil and the blue will not mix. As you tilt the bottle back and forth, you'll see waves rolling gently from one end of the bottle to the other.

When the sun and moon are aligned with each other—during the full and new moon—their gravitational forces work together. This causes stronger-than-usual tides called spring tides. When the moon and sun are at right angles to one another—when we see a half moon—their gravities pull in different directions. This causes weaker neap tides.

If our planet was completely covered with water, the tides would move around the world smoothly and evenly every 12 hours and 25 minutes. But on Earth the height and timing of tides depend on the shape of the shoreline. In some places, there is only a yard (meter) or two of difference between high and low tides. In others, the tidal flow is much greater. The Bay of Fundy in eastern Canada has a shape that funnels the tide in and out. This creates

59

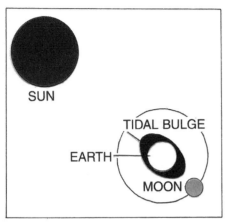

SPRING TIDE

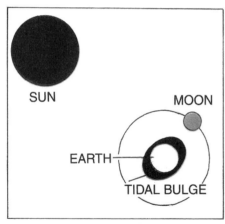

NEAP TIDE

Tides occur as a result of the gravitational forces among Earth, the moon, and the sun.

tides of 45 feet (15 meters)! The tide change is so swift that it causes an actual tidal wave (*not* a tsunami) to race up the St. Johns River as the tide begins to come in.

Because of the shape of the ocean basins, solar tides affect some parts of the ocean more strongly than others. The west coast of Florida is such a place. Rather than two lunar tides each day, Florida's gulf coast has just one solar tide each day. Other places, such as the Pacific coast of the United States, have "mixed" tides. Solar and lunar tides interact to produce one large and one smaller tide change each day.

SEA LEVEL

With the tide rising and falling and waves breaking against the shore, how can we tell where sea level is? The ocean never stays still enough to measure. In fact, "sea level" is really a mean, or average. Scientists measure each low and high tide and then calculate the average for each. Ocean scientists often speak of "mean low water" and "mean high water" instead of sea level.

And these averages change over the years. During the ice ages, more water was frozen in the polar ice caps. So sea level was 320 feet (100 meters) or more lower than it is today. The coastlines of the continents had very different shapes then, too.

In recent years the world's climate has become warmer. Scientists estimate that sea level is now rising at 6 inches (15 centimeters) per century. If global warming continues, more ice caps will melt. This will continue to raise the levels of our oceans, and areas that are now dry land will eventually be underwater.

A MODEL TIDE GAUGE

To measure sea level and tides accurately, scientists must eliminate the effects of the water's motion. To do that, they build a tide gauge.

This measuring device has an inlet that reaches well below the waves, even at the lowest tide. Water inside the gauge isn't affected by the waves that pass by. Here's how to make a model of such a device.

Materials:

5-gallon plastic bucket, 12-inch (30-centimeter) piece of 3- or 4-inch- (7.5- or 10-centimeter-) diameter plastic pipe, 6-inch (15-centimeter) C-clamp, large plastic fishing float, stiff wire (coathanger wire will do), pen, graph paper, cylindrical metal cookie tin, 2 12-inch (30-centimeter) wooden squares cut from 2- by 12-inch (5- by 30-centimeter) board, 1-inch- (2.5-centimeter-) diameter dowel rod, a hammer and some nails, a pair of needle-nose pliers, and tape

Procedure:

Fasten the plastic pipe to the inner wall of the bucket with the clamp, so that the top of the pipe is about 2 inches (5 centimeters) above the top of the bucket.

Cut a 12-inch (30-centimeter) piece of wire. Using the pliers, bend both ends of the wire into loops. Attach the fishing float to one of the loops.

Make the support stands for your device: Saw the dowel rod into one 24-inch (60-centimeter) length and one 22-inch (55 centimeter) length. Drive a large nail all the way through the center of a 2- by 12-inch (5- by 30-centimeter) square. Stand one of the dowels vertically on a hard surface. Center the point of the nail that you drove through the board in the middle of the circular end of the dowel, and drive it into the dowel with the hammer. Repeat this process with the second board and dowel rod.

Your own tide gauge will help you measure water levels in your experiments.

Straighten and cut a 24-inch (60-centimeter) piece of stiff wire. With the pliers, bend a small loop in each end. Then bend a 360-degree loop in the center of the wire.

Put a small nail through the middle loop in the wire. Hammer the nail into the longer dowel rod about 3 inches (7.5 centimeters) below the top. Do not hammer the nail all the way in—the wire should balance horizontally on the stand and swing up and down freely.

Tape a piece of graph paper around the metal cylinder. Hammer a nail through the center of the bottom of the cylinder. Then turn the cylinder upside down over the top of the shorter stand. Nail the cylinder to the center of the dowel. Again, don't hammer the nail all the way in. The cylinder should be able to turn.

Tape the pen into the loop at one end of the long wire. Adjust the position of the stands so the pen touches the graph paper.

Put the fishing float—attached to the shorter wire—into the plastic pipe. Hook the upper end of the short wire into the loop on the other end of the longer wire.

Pour water into the bucket until it is about half full. Position the bucket and stands so the float can move up and down easily in the pipe. You may have to adjust the length of the shorter wire.

Your model tide gauge is now complete. When you change the level of water in the bucket, the plastic float should move up and down. As it does, the pen will record changes in the water level. But when you make waves in the bucket by sloshing the water with your hands, the position of the pen should remain unchanged.

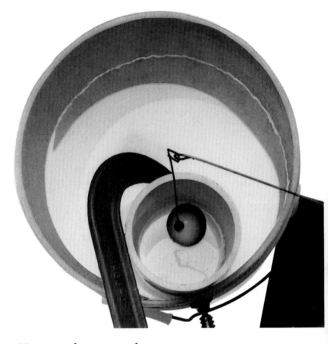

Using a homemade depth gauge is a fun experiment, but be sure to have an adult present at all times.

63

Chapter Six

Undersea Resources

For as long as humans have lived on Earth, the ocean has given us much of what we need to survive. The ocean provides food, salt, minerals, and energy. Seawater can even be processed to produce fresh drinking water. And scientists are still looking for new ways to use marine resources more effectively.

FOOD FROM THE SEA

The ocean is an important source of food. Fisheries supply about 10 percent of the world's animal protein—about 60 million tons of food a year.

In some parts of the world, seafood is the main source of protein. Some kinds of fish are processed into oils and animal feed. Seaweeds are also used as food and food additives.

Unfortunately, humans don't always use the oceans' resources wisely. The world's growing population has put even greater strains on marine food supplies. Important species such as salmon, tuna, and sardines have been badly overfished. If too many fish are harvested, there will not be enough left to breed and replace the ones that have been caught. One recent report says we may have already reached the limit of how much seafood we can gather from the oceans.

Fisheries scientists study the life cycle of each species to find out how quickly it can reproduce and grow. They try to decide how much can be caught each year without reducing future catches. This is called the maximum sustainable yield. But fish behavior is hard to study in the open ocean, and counting the number of a given species is even more difficult. The size of fish populations changes naturally from year to year even without human fishing. So, deciding how much tuna or herring the oceans can produce is a difficult job.

To keep within the maximum sustainable yield, governments put a variety of limits on fishing. Fishers may be allowed to catch only a certain amount of each species. The number of days they may fish or the size of the fish they keep may be controlled. Fishing for threatened species may be stopped completely until their populations recover. Striped bass fishing on the east coast of the United States has been successfully saved by a total ban for a period of time. Unfortunately, some species have been so badly overfished that they may never recover, even with government protections.

FRESH WATER

Only a tiny fraction of the world's water is drinkable. The ocean, which holds 97 percent of the planet's water, is too salty to drink. It is also too salty to use for farming or in industry. The salt would kill most crops and would rust most machinery. But there are ways to change seawater into fresh water. This process is called desalination.

Desalination has become an important source of fresh water in some parts of the world. For example, Saudi Arabia has a desalination plant that makes 250 million gallons (almost 1 billion liters) of fresh water a day.

Salt can be removed from seawater in several ways. The simplest way is to distill the seawater. Seawater is heated, and the water vapor that results is captured and condensed again. The condensed water is fresh and pure.

Another desalination method is called reverse osmosis. In this process, pressurized seawater is forced through a thin sheet of plastic with microscopic holes. The salt is left behind, and only fresh water passes through. Seawater can also be made drinkable by chilling it and then skimming off the nearly salt-free ice that forms at the surface. Still another method, known as electrodialysis, makes use of electric current to desalinate water.

Desalinating large quantities of water requires a lot of energy and expensive equipment. It is most practical in dry, tropical regions where fresh water is scarce and solar energy can be used to power the process.

FRESH WATER WITH A SOLAR STILL

Materials:

A glass loaf pan, a small collecting bowl, clear plastic wrap, tape or a large strong rubber band, salt water, a small, rounded stone

Procedure:

Cut a piece of plastic wrap large enough to fit over the loaf pan, with plenty of overlap on all sides.

Fill the pan with about an inch of salt water. Place the collecting bowl in the center of the pan.

Then cover the entire pan with the plastic wrap. Attach it around the edges of the pan with the tape or rubber band.

Place the pan in a warm, sunny location. Carry the pan carefully so that no salt water splashes into the collecting bowl.

Desalinating water using a solar still takes time but little effort.

Place the small stone in the center of the plastic wrap, just above the collecting bowl. This will let the condensed droplets of fresh water run into the bowl.

Let your solar still sit in the sunshine for several hours. In the evening, after the air has become cooler, carefully remove the plastic and taste the water that has collected in the bowl. It should be perfectly fresh and pure.

SALT AND OTHER MINERALS

Salt is an important nutrient. It's more than a seasoning for our food. Our bodies need at least some salt to live.

When seawater evaporates, what's left is salt. In some parts of the world, people use seawater to make salt for cooking. Seawater is piped into shallow basins and allowed to evaporate. The different chemicals in the water crystallize at different times. By transferring the water from one basin to another as it evaporates, workers remove unwanted chemicals. After the water has evaporated, what remains is almost pure sodium chloride—table salt. Like desalination, this is most practical in hot, dry climates where the sun can provide the power.

As we learned in Chapter One, seawater contains many chemicals besides ordinary salt (sodium chloride). Two of these are concentrated enough to be collected commercially. Most magnesium and bromine are produced from sea salt. Currently it is too expensive to extract other chemicals from seawater.

69

Other mineral resources come from the ocean floor. Construction and roadbuilding projects use huge amounts of sand, gravel, and seashells dredged from the ocean floor. In some coastal areas, runoff from rivers has left concentrations of minerals in the sediments. Gold, tin, chromium, and titanium, as well as sulfur and phosphorus, are all mined from shallow coastal waters.

Mineral resources are also found on the deep ocean floor. Vast fields of stonelike mineral deposits called manganese nodules cover the bottom in parts of the Pacific Ocean. These round nodules contain nickel, copper, iron, and cobalt as well as manganese. Mining these nodules is still an experimental process.

The ocean is so vast that, without a doubt, other valuable mineral resources are still waiting to be discovered.

PETROLEUM AND NATURAL GAS

Petroleum is produced when billions of dead single-celled marine creatures are buried under layers of undersea sediments for millions of years. The remains of these creatures gradually change into oil and gas. So it's not surprising that much of the world's petroleum is produced from undersea wells.

Oil companies set up huge drilling rigs in coastal waters. A number of wells can be drilled from each rig. This kind of drilling is done in the Gulf of Mexico, the North Sea, the Persian Gulf, along the coasts of southern California and Venezuela, and in other coastal waters.

Such drilling is expensive and dangerous work, especially in stormy waters like the North Sea. Oil spills sometimes result as tankers transfer the petroleum from well to refinery. These spills damage beaches and kill marine life. And, of course, petroleum resources are not renewable. Once they're used up, they can't be replaced.

Despite all these problems, our world economy depends so heavily on petroleum products that people are willing to take the risks of undersea drilling.

POWER GENERATION

In addition to supplies of petroleum, the oceans can provide nonpolluting, renewable energy resources. The winds, waves, tides, and heat energy in ocean water can all be harnessed to generate electrical power.

Winds along the coastline are usually steady and reliable because the sun heats land and sea unevenly (see Chapter Four). The seacoast, then, is a good place for wind-powered generators. This is a proven method that is used to make electricity in many places, including coastal California.

In a few places around the world, the difference between high and low tide is so great that the surge of the water can be used to run electrical generators. A dam is built across a narrow tidal channel. The dam holds back the tide as it rises. The water is channeled through turbines. The spinning turbines power generators to produce electricity. When the tide goes out, the water is trapped on the inner side of the dam. It can be used to spin the turbines and make electricity once again.

There are tidal generating stations already operating in France and Russia. Other possible sites include the Bay of Fundy in eastern Canada, with its tidal flow of about 45 feet (15 meters).

Ocean Thermal Energy Conversion (or OTEC) is a method of making electricity that takes advantage of the difference in temperature between warm surface waters and colder deep ocean water.

OTEC works like a home heat pump in reverse. It takes the heat from the ocean and turns it into electrical power. The heat in the surface water vaporizes a liquid chemical refrigerant. The pressure of this gas spins a turbine and generator. Then the deep ocean water cools the refrigerant and condenses it back into a liquid.

OTEC needs a big difference between surface and deep water temperatures year-round. So it is only practical in tropical and subtropical regions. There is a small OTEC generator operating on the island of Hawaii. But Ocean Thermal Energy Conversion is still experimental, however, and power companies are not yet using it to make electricity commercially.

Another experimental method of making electricity uses the constant motion of the ocean's surface. Waves carry tremendous amounts of energy. This up-and-down motion already powers small electrical generators in floating navigational buoys. But scientists have not yet developed practical ways to generate large amounts of electricity from waves.

THE OCEAN AND THE
ECOLOGICAL BALANCE OF THE PLANET

We must all remember how much our lives depend on the ocean. The oceans regulate our weather and provide most of the moisture that falls to Earth as rain. Algae in the upper layers of the ocean make much of the oxygen we breathe and form the base of the food chain that supplies us with food. And, of course, the ocean provides recreation, transportation, and a way to make a living for millions of people around the world.

The marine environment is vast. When we look out on the open ocean, it may seem as if it is much too big to be harmed by anything people can do to it. But human actions can seriously damage the world's oceans if we're not careful. If we overharvest its fish or use the ocean as a dump for harmful wastes, we put our own lives at risk, too. The ocean is a precious resource that human beings must learn to treasure and protect.

Find Out More About the Ocean

Adler, David. *Our Amazing Ocean*. Mahwah, New Jersey: Troll Associates, 1983.

Blair, Carvel. *Exploring the Sea: Oceanography Today*. New York: Random House, 1986.

Bramwell, Martyn. *The Oceans*. New York: Franklin Watts, 1987.

Bright, Michael. *The Dying Sea*. New York: Franklin Watts, 1992.

Center for Marine Conservation Staff, *The Ocean Book: Aquarium and Seaside Activities and Ideas for All Ages*. New York: John Wiley and Sons, 1989.

The Facts On File Dictionary of Marine Science. New York: Facts On File, 1988.

Gibbs, B., *Ocean Facts*. Tulsa: Usborne, 1991.

Gilbreath, Alice. *River in the Ocean: The Story of the Gulf Stream*. Minneapolis: Dillon Press, 1986.

Hare, Tony. *Polluting the Sea*. London and New York: Gloucester Press, 1990.

Johnson, Rebecca L. *Diving Into Darkness: A Submersible Explores the Sea*. Minneapolis: Lerner, 1989.

Kovacs, Deborah. *A Day Underwater*. New York: Scholastic, 1987.

Lambert, David. *The Oceans*. New York: The Bookwright Press, 1984.

Lambert, David, and Anita McConnell. *Seas And Oceans*. New York: Facts On File, 1985.

Lye, Keith. *The Ocean Floor*. New York: Franklin Watts, 1991.

Myerson, A. Lee. *Seawater: A Delicate Balance*. Hillside, NJ: Enslow, 1988.

Nixon, Hershell H. and Joan Lowery. *Land Under the Sea*. New York: Dodd, Mead, 1985.

Pearce, Querida Lee. *Tidal Waves and Other Ocean Wonders*. New York: Simon and Schuster, 1989.

Poynter, Margaret, and Donald Collins. *Under the High Seas: New Frontiers in Oceanography*. New York: Atheneum, 1983.

The Random House Atlas of the Oceans. New York: Random House, 1991.

Reef, Catherine. *Jacques Cousteau: Champion of the Sea*. Frederick, MD: Twenty-first Century Books, 1992.

Rogers, Mary M. *Our Endangered Planet: Oceans*. Minneapolis: Lerner, 1991.

Simon, Seymour. *How to Be an Ocean Scientist in Your Own Home.* New York: J.B. Lippincott, 1988.

———. *Oceans.* New York: Morrow Junior Books, 1990.

Souza, Dorothy M. *Powerful Waves.* Minneapolis: Carolrhoda Books, 1992.

Tesar, Jenny. *Threatened Oceans.* New York: Facts On File, 1992.

Twist, Clint. *Seas and Oceans.* New York: Dillon, 1991.

Waters, John F. *Deep-Sea Vents: Living Worlds Without Sun.* New York: Dutton, 1994.

Wells, Susan. *The Illustrated World of Oceans.* New York: Simon and Schuster, 1993.

Whitfield, Philip. *Oceans.* New York: Viking, 1991.

Yardley, Thompson. *Make a Splash! Care About the Ocean.* Brookfield, Conn.: The Millbrook Press, 1992.

Index